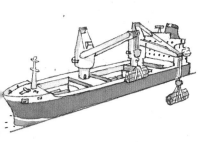

Learning Points

- *Things That Go* is designed to help you to introduce children to simple facts about moving vehicles and methods of transport.

- Children are fascinated by anything that travels overland or in the air, and it's exciting for them to be able to recognise and learn more about these vehicles in their own books.

- Take time to look at the details in the pictures and to talk about them. Which vehicles has your child seen? What can he or she remember about them?

- Next time you go on a walk together, see if you can spot some things that go!

Ladybird books are widely available, but in case of difficulty may be ordered by post or telephone from:

Ladybird Books – Cash Sales Department
Littlegate Road Paignton Devon TQ3 3BE
Telephone 01803 554761

A catalogue record for this book is available
from the British Library

Published by Ladybird Books Ltd Loughborough Leicestershire UK
Ladybird Books Inc Auburn Maine 04210 USA

let's look at
Things
That Go

by Karen Bryant-Mole
illustrated by Norman Young

Ladybird

Cars

Cars take people to lots of
different places.
What places have you been to
in a car?

Where do you think the children in this car might have been?

Buses

Buses are big and carry lots of passengers. They can take people on short trips or long journeys.

This bus is taking children to school. One little boy is running because he is late!
Have you ever been on a bus?

Trucks

This truck has come to a factory to pick up boxes of tinned fruit. When the boxes are loaded, the truck driver will take them to the local supermarket.

A forklift truck lifts the boxes.
Can you count how many are
waiting to be loaded?

Motorbikes

Motorbikes have two wheels with an engine fixed between them. They can go very fast.

These riders are all wearing
special helmets.
Do you know what they are called?

Aeroplanes

This huge aeroplane is called a jumbo jet. It is going to take off and fly the passengers to a far away country.

Can you see the baggage being loaded onto the plane?

Bikes and Trikes

It's great fun riding around the park on a bike or a trike!
A bike has two wheels and a trike has three wheels.

Which is the bike and which is
the trike?

Helicopters

Helicopters fly high above fields and towns. Sometimes helicopters are used to rescue people who are in trouble.

The people in this helicopter have rescued a climber who has hurt his leg. Can you see him?

Removal Vans

When people move house they hire a removal van to take the furniture to their new home.

These removal men are busy
moving a kitchen table.
Can you see what else they have
put in the van?

Trains

Trains run along railway tracks, making a clickety-clack sound. The passengers get on and off at stations.

How many passengers are getting
off at this train station?

Fire Engines

A fire engine's flashing light and wailing siren warn people that it is on its way to a fire. These firefighters have been called to put out a house fire.

What do you think the ladder on top of the fire engine is used for?

Ships

Some ships carry cargo, like food, oil or wood. Others carry passengers. This cargo ship is being loaded with logs.

How are the logs being lifted on board?

Camper Vans

This family is on holiday in their camper van.

Camper vans have cookers and beds, so people can eat and sleep in them.

Camper vans are like small houses on wheels! Who is asleep in the shade?